## Disclaimers

This book is presented to you for informational purposes only and is not a substitution for any professional advice. The contents herein are based on the views and opinions of the author and all associated contributors.

While every effort has been made by the author and all associated contributors to present accurate and up to date information within this document, it is apparent technologies rapidly change. Therefore, the author and all associated contributors reserve the right to update the contents and information provided herein as these changes progress. The author and/or all associated contributors take no responsibility for any errors or omissions if such discrepancies exist within this document.

The author and all other contributors accept no responsibility for any consequential actions taken, whether monetary, legal, or otherwise, by any and all readers of the materials provided. It is the reader's sole responsibility to seek professional advice before taking any action on their part.

Readers results will vary based on their skill level and individual perception of the contents herein, and thus no guarantees, monetarily or otherwise, can be made accurately. Therefore, no guarantees are made.

## Two Web Marketing Books Inside:

- Quickly Dominate Social Media Marketing: The Ultimate Guide Top Tips to Pinterest, Google+, Facebook, Twitter, Instagram, LinkedIn and YouTube Viral Marketing.

- SEO: Search Engine Optimization - Quickly Learn How to Dominate the Search Engines and What You Need to Know About the Google Panda and Penguin.

This book takes a look at Search Engine Optimization and Online Marketing.

# Small Business: Quick and Easy Guide to Marketing, Business and the Digital Generation - 2 Book Bundle

## By

## Amanda Eliza Bertha

Quickly Dominate Social Media Marketing:
The Ultimate Guide Top Tips to Pinterest,
Google+, Facebook, Twitter, Instagram,
LinkedIn and YouTube Viral Marketing

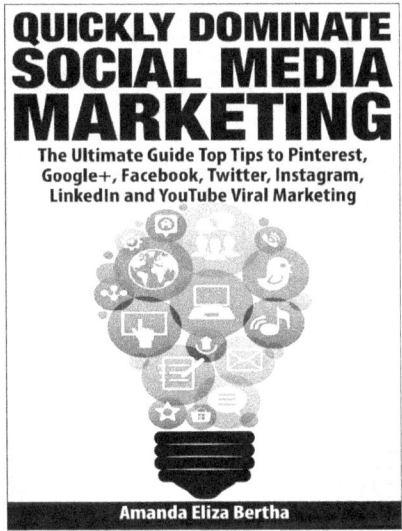

## The Ultimate Guide Top Tips

This guide is to the big names in social media marketing. These are the big three – Facebook, Twitter and Pinterest in that order, followed by Google+, Instagram, LinkedIn and YouTube. According to some reports at the end of 2012, the numbers for these social media marketing sites were:

- Facebook – 1 billion

- Twitter – 500 million

- Pinterest – 25 million

- Google+ – 400 million

- Instagram – 100 million

- LinkedIn – 175 million

- YouTube – 800 million

Another site measures popularity differently. According to it, in August 2012, the unique monthly visitor count was this:

- Facebook – 750 million

- Twitter – 250 million

- LinkedIn – 110 million

- Google+ – 65 million estimated

Another site reports Pinterest as having 120 million visitors a month. This is why Pinterest is listed as number 3 above. Also it has the reputation as the fastest growing social media site.

The message is, regardless of the ranking, social media is huge. Nothing in the history of the world has brought people together and changed the face of business like social media has.

This guide offer top tips to the primary social media marketing sites. But first let's look at the concept of viral marketing.

# Viral Marketing

Reveal Yourself

The days of setting up a website and going professional are over. Success online has become more related to the personality of the marketer. The twentieth century image of the successful business person involved the woman in the power suit and the man in a three piece suit. When the new model of entrepreneurship emerged, this was the model that we were following.

When a person can live in a single room and create an online presence with a glitzy website and glossy photos, it becomes clear that the system could possibly be open to scams. As web users got savvier, so did the ways of creating online personas.

When the web 2.0 world, or the social media world, began to develop, it grew at amazing rates. A decade ago, there was not even a hint of something like Facebook or Twitter, not to mention all the other social marketing sites.

Brick and mortar businesses still operated, for the most part separate from internet businesses. People who knew the internet world well could discern the genuine opportunities online, for the most part. That was then, this is now.

A lot has changed. Social media has become an incredible peer-to-peer experience for everyone from children to senior citizens. With a billion people on Facebook and apparently four billion visiting YouTube a month, the potential reach of viral marketing is astounding.

Note: If you do a search, you will find that the numbers vary but all sites agree that there are huge numbers visiting daily. You cannot easily capture the attention of everyone out there but you can certainly carve out a niche for yourself and spread your message to increasingly large numbers of people.

In other words, the time is now and the free tools are there for you to use. All you need is your own personal toolkit.

## Overview

Whether you use all of these social media sites or just a few of them, you need a toolkit. There is more to viral marketing than setting up a Facebook page. Unfortunately too many people start with the tools but without a toolkit.

This might be disappointing news for you if you were looking for a fast and easy way to hit the market and go viral but there is no set of quick tricks that will help you get ahead in any of these social media sites. For a long time, there were a lot of internet marketing gurus touting ways to get followers, likes or shares or whatever the measurement of success was on a social media site.

The sites kept ahead of these systems and while some of the schemes would work for a while, when the social media system changed, all that work went down the drain.

Instead, this guide will talk about the best methods to use in each social media site to reach out to the great network of potentially interested people out there.

You will notice that for the most part, the sections don't get into details about how to sign up, join or work with the tools in the site. The reason for this is that things keep changing. By the time this book hits the marketplace, the site may have already changed its layout and location of the buttons and forms.

So these are two things that are not covered – how to get around doing the work and the technical details of registering as a member of a site.

## The Toolkit

This is the hardest part of the whole process and it takes some serious concentration. Here is the first step:

Your Goal: Successful Viral Marketing

Your Message: [Fill in the blank]

What is the message? What are you selling? Suppose you are an affiliate marketer – what are you selling? Health food supplements, technology, relationship advice?

There is an old Calvin and Hobbes cartoon where Calvin has set up a stand with the sign "A Swift Kick in the Butt - $1.00" and the caption shows Calvin telling Hobbes, "Everybody I know needs what I'm selling!"

Calvin is right, maybe. But the real thing is, does everybody want a swift kick in the butt. You challenge is to find a way to make people believe that not only do they need your product or service but they want it.

If you are an affiliate marketer who focuses on being a marketer and who promotes a variety of products, you have to consider the effort in promoting yourself as an expert in a variety of topics or find a common thread and focus on that.

If you have an offline business and you want to promote it online, you need to transform your offline message into online lingo.

Your goal is to sum up your message in one sentence. Preferably a short sentence.

This will be the hook for all your marketing efforts in social media.

Once you have this message encapsulated, you can begin to build your toolkit.

Here are the primary components in your toolkit:

- #Hashtags
- Profile Details
- Photos and images

Rather than reinvent the wheel as you set up your online profiles on these social media sites, you need to have a folder ready to go with the photos and images you plan to use, a list of hashtags ready to copy and paste, and a prepared document with your details ready to add to your profile.

Keep adding to this file with new information and images so that you are never lost for words when you are online. This helps streamline the process of setting up or revamping your existing social media entities. It also helps create a consistency from one site to another.

## Your Business Plan

You need a plan. The very phrase business plan strikes terror into the heart of many business people. This does have to be a huge task. All you need to do is:

1.     Create your one sentence description of your product or service.

2.     Build your toolkit.

3.     Build an online presence – also known as your website.

4.     Choose your social media sites.

5.     Set up your presence on each site.

6.     Develop a posting plan for each site.

7.     Schedule time for your posts.

8.     Implement your posting plan.

One of the problems is that people think that it will only take a few minutes to post and they figure that they can squeeze that in sometime during the day.

This is a flaw that is pretty close to fatal for your plan. Something happens – the phone rings or someone drops into your office or you have an email that cannot be ignored or you sleep in – and you think that you will post tomorrow. If this happens too often, you will fall behind and never go viral.

It is better to set a posting schedule that really can be done in a few minutes and alternate the days that you post on each site. Or better yet set up posts that can jump from one social media site to another. For instance, you can have your Facebook posts tweeted. And vice versa.

One example of a great integrative tool for linking your social media is Tweetdeck (http://tweetdeck.com). You can add Facebook, Twitter and LinkedIn to Tweetdeck and manage all of these from one console on your computer. If you have several accounts in each of these places, you can add all of them and handle them all at once.

However, this is a way of posting from one location to these three sites. You really want to set up a linkage that lets one post appear on other sites at the same time.

Until the middle of 2012, you were able to have your tweets and LinkedIn work together but the relationship ended. It is the nature of social media channels to change. However, a solution has emerged – Buffer (http://bufferapp.com/)

You can use Woobox (http://woobox.com/pinterest) to have your Pinterest pins appear on Facebook. And then there is Extended Share for Google+ which allows you to share your Google+ post with your Twitter, Facebook, LinkedIn and Pinterest accounts.

These are just a few examples of how you can link your social media channels together. And don't worry about overwhelming the world with the same message coming at them from a bunch of different places. The same advertising wisdom still holds – a person has to see your name seven times before that person registers you in their memory.

Have you ever bought a new car and suddenly you see so many cars just like yours? Have you ever heard a phrase and then hear it again the same day, maybe a couple of times? This is because your brain has become attuned to that type of car or that phrase. Think of your social media world as a way of bringing your product or service to the forefront of peoples' minds.

Regardless of which social media channel you are in, do not just post links to your sales page. There are Twitter folk who do this. They will post six times a day but all they post is a direct link to their sales page.

Yawn.

Not appealing. Even the best written sales page in the world is not going to win the hearts and minds of people like entertainment does. Think of the winning ads you see on television. They often tell a story to capture your attention.

For years now, the value of a well written and psychologically compelling sales page has been touted as the route to success and in reality, it is still valuable but a masterpiece is useless if no one gets there to read it.

It is impossible to create a viral marketing meme that will hit the public's imagination with some sort of formula. For instance, one of the top memes for 2012 was Grumpy Cat. Including Grumpy Cat here in this book is a way that the cat, whose real name is Tartar Sauce, can go even more viral but this is not a business meme.

This is a cat who became famous when his owner's brother posted his picture on Reddit. Grumpy Cat hit the big time because there was something in the kitty's demeanor that appealed to people.

The example of Grumpy Cat is just to show you why you need to round up as many interesting images as you can and the value of using your own photos (or your sister's) in your viral marketing.

Given a choice between reading a sales page or sharing this cranky-looking cat's picture, well, apparently many people choose the cat.

The days of the serious looking gentleman in his tailored suit convincing you to buy his {fill in the blank with whatever you are trying to sell} are gone and in the twenty-first century, the iconic business person has a bit of a geeky image. The ultimate online presence has a touch of geek and a touch of everyday humor and a touch of compassion for the world.

Some of the following social media channels are so new that they are still shaping themselves. The "viewing audience" is a bright and engaged bunch out there and the relationship between the marketer and the end user is much different than it ever was before.

In a larger and more virtual world, we have come back to the old country farmer's market where you display your wares in the best possible way and try to reach out to people who see you as a real human being not someone who is going to sell you day old pies just to make a few bucks.

## Pinterest

Ben Silbermann, Paul Sciarra, and Evan Sharp came up with the concept of Pinterest began in December 2009. They launched it in March 2010. If you were online then, you might remember that you had to be invited to join Pinterest.

A year later, there was an iPhone app for Pinterest and that dramatically increased the number of users. By December 2011, Pinterest hit the top 10 list for the largest social network services. By January 2012, it was sending more referral traffic than LinkedIn, YouTube, and Google+. It holds the record for being the fastest site to break through the 10 million unique visitor spot.

Pinterest is an online pin board and it is based on images that are sorted by categories. People love images and can add something that they like based on the image on that page or they can create their own pin using their own images.

If you want to use Pinterest (and it is highly recommended that you do – having a potential audience of at least 4 million people a day is pretty awesome), here are the top tips for maximizing the benefits of Pinterest.

1.     Use images on your pages. Make the images as appealing as possible and of course, make sure that you are not violating any copyrights. If you have appealing images with the proper permissions, other people can easily pin your page to their boards. On Pinterest you have three options: Add a Pin, Upload a Pin, and Create a Board. Many people just add a pin but they need both your web address and an image on the web page so they can pin your page to their board.

2.     If you want to add your own chosen image on your computer, choose the right topic for your new pin and add a note but also remember to add a link to the site you are promoting. It is possible and too easy to just add the image and comment. This might be pleasant for people to look at but it does not help you market your site.

3.    Choose the right category. If you just guess at the category to use and you are wrong, you might not reach the right audience for your pins.

4.    When you create a board, allow others to post to your board. The default is "Just Me". You can change it to "Me + Contributors." You have to follow at least one of your contributor's boards but this lets you share the load with someone else you trust.

5.    Find great images. Once again, be sure you are not violating copyright. The easiest way to find huge numbers of great images is by searching for "images creative commons" plus your topic. You can also search Google Images for creative commons images. Another super source for creative commons images is Flickr.com. And of course, you can also search for images that are public domain. Credit the source. It's only polite.

6.    Pin videos. Find them the same way that you find images or combine Pinterest with another great viral marketing tool – YouTube.

7.    Link your pin to Facebook, but pin it to the Facebook Timeline because this makes it easier for Facebook users to find your pin which they can then repin.

8.    Edit your Pinterest profile. The Edit profile button is in the middle of the page. Look below your picture. Also, while you are there, find the Facebook and Twitter settings and in the oval box, slide the red slider button to turn on these options. You might as well share your pins with everyone in the Facebook option.

9.    Add a Follow Me on Pinterest button to your website.

10.   Sign up to Zoomsphere (http://www.zoomsphere.com) which lets you check on Pinterest pins and pinners as well as other social media sites. You sign up with your Facebook or Twitter account. This is an analytic source for details by date.

11.   Avoid efforts to game the system on Pinterest. Pinterest users are quick to spot a

scam and trying to trick people will not win friends or influence followers.

12.   Be consistent and use the same logo, colors and catch phrases so that people will recognize your pins.


## Additional Advice

Find a consistent source of photos and images and have them on hand. Keep checking for new and interesting pictures. While there are free sites available or sites that offer free samples, you need to look deeper and find a source that is not being used by everyone.

You want to stand out from the crowd and yet have images that reflect your persona and your product and services. You also have to credit the sources unless you own the photos and images. The best places to find all the images you will ever need:

1.      Take photos all the time and keep only the ones that are clear and crisp. You do not

have to be a genius photographer but the photos should be bright and appealing.

2.      Use Flickr's Creative Commons feature which is found at http://www.flickr.com/creativecommons/. There are literally millions of good photos there on thousands, if not millions of topics. Most of these millions of photos can be used in return for acknowledging where you got the image.

3.      Search for public domain photos.

Build up a folder full of photos and use them liberally on your blog or website. Pin them. Let other people pin them. In this busy world, one photo really is worth a thousand words.

On Pinterest, the most popular categories are Home, Arts and Crafts, Style and Fashion, Food and Inspiration/Education. Food is the most frequently repinned Style and Fashion

Some Final Bits of Pinterest Advice

- 80% of pins are repins

- Etsy is the most popular source for pins

- Your Amazon affiliate link will be replaced by Pinterest's affiliate link

- No matter how many pins you have on a board, only five will appear.

## Google+

Google+ is different. It does not have the interactivity factor that is as engaging as Facebook's interactivity factor. Yet, it has grown to be huge. Some reports say that it is number 3 on the list of social media sites, beating out Pinterest.

Even though there is a way of measuring the metrics, social media is a fast moving target. In talking about Google+, there are two guiding principles that apply. These are:

Post frequently. Keep strutting your stuff on Google+. Don't only post to sell something. Offer links of value and words of value and do it often. Frequently can be a subjective term but it means more than once a month. People will forget you if they don't hear from you a lot. If you want a figure for what is considered a good rate of frequency, think about posting three times a week.

Use rich media. Videos and striking images are great because they will encourage other people to share your posts.

Do these two things and you will be able to benefit from the magic of Google+ – which is that Google+ belongs to Google which means that Google+ entries tend to be loved by Google. While this is a short set of tips for using Google+, they are crucial.

Focusing on one type of social media is like trying to fly with one wing. Spread your wings and hit the big media sites. Be interesting, be frequent, be noticed. Hook your other social media events to Google+ and reach out to more readers who will shared your posts whether they are on Facebook, Twitter, Pinterest, or any of the other sites described here.

### Top Tips for Google+ Success

Focus on your profile. The Google+ wisdom is that the difference between an okay profile and a great profile is about an hour of work. Because you have your profile set up in your toolkit, this might take you less than an hour.

Share all the great things that you find. A classic mistake is wanting to keep all the good information for ourselves so that our competitors don't also find out about this great idea. That is completely backwards thinking. The more you share, the more people will appreciate your research abilities and turn to you for more great bits of information.

Add the Google+ badge to your blog or website so people can click on your badge while they are still pumped up from reading your great blog.

Use hashtags. You can even use them in comments in Google+. This makes it easier to find related topics.

Build a circle and the theme you have stored in the tool kit. Hashtag the circle theme and go on a search for people with similar interests and invite them you're your circle. Share the circle and watch the viral love grow.

Reach out and offer advice to other people on Google+ even if the topic is not in your area of expertise. If it is something you know about or can find out something about it, be sociable.

## Facebook

Facebook uses a system called EDGERank to determine how far a reach your Facebook page will have. It is a combination of popularity X relevance X recency. Popularity is measured by the number of likes, shares and comments that your posts get, relevancy is how pertinent your fans think your posts are and of course, recency is how new the post is.

Guess what this means?

Yes. You have to update your fan page often with something that is relevant to your topic and you have to have people interacting and sharing.

Without these factors, your Facebook page will never leap into the viral aspect of marketing. Speaking of marketing, it is not a matter of being subtle but of being personable. Don't go posting direct sales links all the time. Once a week, you might be able to sneak in a direct link to a sales page but more than that, people will not be entertained.

Worse than that, Facebook itself will not be amused. They want Facebook to be a friendly place not a sales pitch place that ends up looking like a middle of the night infomercial.

**Tips for viral marketing with Facebook:**

Post often.

Be interesting.

Don't be all about making sales.

Be personal with people and respond to their posts.

Ways to get people to share your posts:

Use funny photos with captions.

Create amusing videos and upload them to YouTube and share them on Facebook.

Post a poll.


**Twitter**

Learn to speak in 140 characters. It's good for you and will teach you to communicate well.

People land on any site and give it about 2 seconds to capture their interest before they leave. Using Twitter is good practice in being concise. It focuses your concepts and this helps when you add something to your website or blog.

It's also great for learning how to write catchy ads that usually have narrow limits like Google AdWords which allows you 25 words to catch a potential buyer's attention.

One of the secrets to building a presence online is having a consistent and frequent forum for your words. If you have ever tried to maintain a blog you know how hard it is to find new, fresh and interesting content.

Twitter is a great way to get into the habit of posting online. For some people, it might be all that they need to do to get their message out.

There is something that should be addressed here and that is the pressure to write is difficult, even for writers and people who love to write. On Twitter, you can avoid that particular pressure because you have to keep the word count very low.

If you are thinking about how hard it is to sell online in a few words, there is another important thing you need to know. It is more important to connect with people than it is to be an authority in your niche. This is the way that the internet has developed. People love peer-to-peer socialization and have become weary of the websites filled with tons of hard-hitting copy sales pushing them to buy.

Socialization isn't about information. It's about connecting with other people. And you can connect via Twitter any time without needing great chunks of time.

With Twitter these are the tips that will help you spread the word about what your passion is:

Think of Tweeting as a form of texting. Make it short, punchy and informative. Use Twitter like an electronic Post-It™ note. You're busy building a business and you friends who are your readers are overwhelmed with messages. Make it clear and easy to understand.

Use your Twitter personal profile page to tell people who you are. If you are active and engaging on Twitter, people will get curious and want to know more about you. Link to your blog and website. Don't make it pure marketing – the point is to get people to like you and your messages, not to oversell and push them away.

Use hashtags. This is just a simple matter of adding a key word with a hash mark (#) in front of it.

Put a picture on your Twitter profile. People want to see who you are.

Do not check the "Protect My Updates" box. If you do check this box, your profile and links will be hidden from people and that defeats the purpose of being on Twitter.

And the biggest tip of all: post at least one update a day. Two is better. You have to get noticed to have people follow you and read your tweets. To get noticed, you have to be out there communicating.

### Instagram

People usually think that Instagram is just a place for uploading pictures. But it is more than that. It's a social platform where you can interact with others. You can comment on other people's photos. Check to see who has commented on your pictures and be sure to reply to them.

Because you are promoting a particular product or service, use photos that relate to whatever you are offering but don't make it too much of a sales pitch. Use this photo-oriented place to show how your business works.

## Tips for Instagram

The big tip for using Instagram to reach out to the world is to use a hashtag. All this means is to add # before the word that is good to describe your Instagram posts. For instance if you are selling probiotics, you could use #probiotics. It's not exclusive to you but if someone is interested and goes searching #probiotics they will find you. All you need to do is add your hashtag or tags to the caption area.

Upload your photos between 5 and 6 p.m. Posting them at bedtime is not a good idea because people are going to bed too, not checking their Instagram. But around 5 p.m., many people are done work for the day and will check their social network around that time.

## LinkedIn

LinkedIn has a reputation as a business site but it is an ideal social media site. The crowd is just a little different there because they tend to be business people. There is something else about LinkedIn that is different and that is, it is not entirely free. You can have an account for free but it is limited. If you want to expand your reach in LinkedIn, you can upgrade to a paid account which allows you to:

- Contact anyone directly

- Find more profiles

- See full profiles of anyone in your network

- See who's viewed your profile

- Use Profile Organizer to save profiles and notes

- Create automatic searches

- See names of your 3rd degree and Group connections

- Get introduced to the companies you're targeting

- Use Reference Search to get information on anyone

- Use OpenLink to let anyone message you for free

Build your profile, join groups, use LinkedIn for what it is intended to be used for – networking. You can follow the Company Buzz component so you will be up to date on the buzz in your industry.

**Top Tips for LinkedIn**

Use hashtags.

Set up a company page.

Participate in is the Answers feature which lets you display your niche expertise in your niche.

Expand your LinkedIn network with tools such as the Slideshare Presentations application. You can use it to showcase presentations about your products or services.

Build a great profile page that is linked to your business presence online. Let people get to know who you are, what your products do and how you can help them.

## YouTube

On YouTube, you have a golden opportunity to reach a audience. There are a couple of technical things that can help – well one technical thing that can make or break you. Sound. The video itself does need to be clear. With the handy dandy tools that allow you to capture video, this is less of a problem than sound.

Listen to 10 YouTube Videos at random just for the sound. Is there a hum and buzz on the sound track? Is the sound too low? Is it muffled? Is it full of snap and crackles?

If you have a video and the sound is terrible, fix it. Either reshoot the video or do a new sound track and replace the bad one on the video with the better track.

Aside from this technical tip, follow this formula. Tell people what the video is about and present your message. People are on YouTube looking for answers to their questions. They don't want to know how long you have been building computers, they want to know how to get the bottom panel off their laptop.

Keep it short. Keep it informational. Don't violate copyright.

If you don't have a lot of technical knowledge or equipment for creating videos, you can use your smart phone video ability or your computer's webcam and microphone to create a video. Here are some basic tips:

Be yourself but tidy up your appearance a bit – unless you want to be known as the marketer who wears pajamas, put on some day clothes.

Check to make sure your face shows in the camera.

Turn off the television and other sources of noise in the room.

Smile and speak clearly.

Embed your website address in the video so that when it does get shared all over the place, your URL is part of it.

Introduce yourself or close your video with your name (or company name) just to get people used to hearing the name.

The reality of your life might make some of these a challenge. There is one person who does YouTube videos at least once a day and she has been known to even take her laptop to the library so she could have internet access and do her video there. It was difficult to hear her because she had to keep her voice down. But she mentioned that in her video and it was clear that she was in the library.

Her dedication to getting her word out is impressive. And most of her videos have better sound quality so this is not typical of her usual quality.

A common vision is the guy in the shirt with his flip chart pacing the front of a room with lots of hand gestures. It is a typical presentation style and if this is a videotape of a live presentation, then it is understandable.

However, sometimes people stage these videos so that they are appearing to be presenting live. I works for some people but it can verge on looking phony so be careful. Sitting quietly at a desk is an alternate idea that might work just as well or better.

Also, watch your colorful language. Sprinkling swear words and f-bombs throughout your presentation might reflect your personal style but it could prevent a viewer from sharing the video on his or her site because they don't want their viewers to hear some of these words.

## Conclusion

Going viral is a dream and a goal and it is possible, However, bear in mind that there are literally billions of other people out there in the social media world and many of them are also trying to make their mark in the world.

Not all of them are marketing though. Many of them are looking for that special something that will amuse them, entertain them, improve their lives or change their ways of doing things.

Your desire is to reach these people. But first, you have to know who they are. Imagine the typical person who would be interested in your topic and write as if you are writing to that person.

Be passionate and be interested and be open-minded about feedback. Not all of your posts and comments will be winners and not all will go viral. However, if you write something that appeals to even one of your online friends, that friend will retweet or share or somehow pass it along to his friends and maybe one of them will pass it on and then two more people will pass it on and so it goes.

If this happens once, it will happen again and someday soon, someone who has seen this shared on Facebook will say, oh it's that company again. I remember them and they have interesting posts.

Then the next time they see one of your posts, they might go looking to find out more about you. This is where they will find one of your detailed profiles.

Become personal and yet work on a schedule. Reach out to the world and get them to like you (on Facebook) and you are on your way.

## SEO: Search Engine Optimization - Quickly Learn How to Dominate the Search Engines and What You Need to Know About the Google Panda and Penguin

Introduction

Rather than go into a long explanation, here is a brief bit of background to the introduction of the World Wide Web to the general population. The reason for this is that without understanding how the internet developed, it is difficult to grasp the situation where seeking page one of Google means so much to the web business world.

To begin at the beginning we have to go back to 1980 when Tim Berners-Lee came up with the concept of hypertext as a way to share information. It was hard for scientists to share ideas across the country because they were limited to text and much of their exploration involved drawings and sketches. Eventually, Berners-Lee realized that the power of sharing information would increase immensely if he could find a way to share the information using the protocols that had become available for sharing communications.

Actually, the internet concept had been in use since the Bay of Pigs invasion in 1961 when the American government realized that having all their command information in one location was very dangerous. A single hit could wipe out communications and cripple the country.

Here is a tiny bit of background on the Bay of Pigs Invasion. It was an April 1961 invasion of Cuba carried out by Brigade 2506. This Brigade was a militia group that the CIA paid for and trained. The plan was for the Brigade to overthrow the Cuban government ruled by Osvaldo Dorticós Torrado. However, the CIA-trained Brigade 2506 was defeated by a Cuban army led by Cuba's Prime Minister Fidel Castro. This defeat was a shock to the American government and focused attention on the need to protect the country in the Cold War that had been underway for several years.

With the possibility of more defeat, with communist Cuba hovering so close to the country, there was an acute awareness of a serious problem. What if the communication system was destroyed completely? And it could be because there was one central core to the communications. Brilliant scientists at the top universities studied the problem. Leonard Kleinrock, a graduate student at MIT, had discovered something called packet switching and in 1961, he wrote a paper about it.

Very simply stated, packet switching means that messages are divided up into packets that are sent in little pieces and when the packets all arrive at their destination, they are reunited. This was the heart of the solution to centralized communications. The US government's defense research department set up the ARPAnet (Advanced Research Projects Agency Network) which was built on using packet switching. ARPAnet was the grandfather of the Internet as we know it.

Because ARPAnet connected universities and research centers, it became a way for researchers to share their information and this is why Berners-Lee was looking for a faster and more comprehensive way to share information over the network. His search for a way to share information led to the development of hypertext markup language (HTML) and then a browser that allowed people to see the graphics and details of the research carried out at other institutions. His first browser was the NeXTStep WorldWideWeb application which he created in 1990. On August 6, 1991, Berners-Lee presented the first web page ever to the world. It was the CERN (European Organization for Nuclear Research) site.

However this book is about search engine optimization and it is time to move to the web as we know it today and how search engines came to be so powerful and why Google keeps changing its algorithms.

## The World Wide Web Emerges

The power of html and this method of sharing information exploded on the academic community and spread out to the general population. NeXTStep WorldWideWeb was renamed Nexus and Berners-Lee released the source code into the public domain in 1993. You could edit the hypertext and view it with Nexus. The next browsers developed only allowed people to view the hypertext.

People began to build their own websites. MTV had one of the first websites, appearing in 1993. By the end of 1994, there were about ten thousand websites in the entire world. In 1995, a new website emerged and that was Jerry's Guide to the World Wide Web. Later it changed its name to Yahoo and then to Yahoo!

Yahoo! was the creation of Jerry Yang and David Filo, graduate students in electrical engineering at Stanford. They came up with the idea in January 1994, It was incorporated on March 1, 1995. As the number of website grew so quickly, Yang and Filo came up with the idea of creating a directory and registered the domain name yahoo.com on January 18, 1995.

In case you are wondering about the name, Yahoo stands for Yet Another Hierarchical Officious Oracle. However, yahoo was a common epithet for rural people from the South and Filo was from the southern USA.

The problem began right about this time as the number of web pages grew, it was becoming harder and harder to find what you wanted online. There was more and more information and it was becoming a real challenge to find your way through the mass of pages. Yahoo! was just what people needed to help them find their way through the web.

## Google Begins

In 1995 Sergey Brin and Larry Page met. Page had just graduated from the University of Michigan and Brin was showing him around Stanford. When Page did decide to enter Stanford, he and Brin collaborated on a search engine. They were both computer science graduate students and the World Wide Web was in full flight. They called their project BackRub at first. Then they decided it needed a better name so chose Googol. Googol refers to a very large number – 1 with 100 zeroes. A million has nine zeroes so you can imagine how large this number is.

The two men were only in their early twenties at the time and you can see the playful nature of their naming conventions, just as with Yahoo! This may have been serious stuff but these were students playing with an idea. They planned to systematize all the information on the World Wide Web. The domain googol.com was already taken and rather than deal with the problem of trying to obtain that name, the men chose to register google.com. In September 1998, Page and Brin opened their Google office in Menlo Park in a garage. Within months, the superior algorithm of Google showed its impact on the search engine world. By the end of 2001, Google had three billion documents in its index.

## SEO Explained

This has been a longish explanation of search engines but in order to understand search engine optimization or SEO, it helps to understand the rapid growth of the World Wide Web and the need for people to find ways to have their websites land at the top page of search engines, in particular Google.

Google ruled the Ethernet waves. On one side of the search engine world there were (and are) people like Berners-Lee, Yang, Filo, Page, Brin and a whole legion of similar technical minds whose goal was to make sharing information relevant and accessible.

On the other side of the World Wide Web universe, there were (and are) the entrepreneurs and marketers and web gurus whose goals include being easily found online. If they could discover the perfect way to optimize their websites for search engine optimization, they could be at the top of the list of websites that any search engine found for web surfers.

## SEO – The Early Years

In the early years of search engines, there were also early years of SEO. Think of the growth of search engines and the growth of ways to attract search engines as a kind of dance. On one hand, brilliant minds are trying to find a way to evaluate and reveal the good web pages that are appearing in increasing numbers on the web. On the other hand, the people putting up the growing numbers of web sites are trying to figure out how to make their web pages appear at the top of the directory lists.

Since the whole concept is very new and constantly changing, the algorithms are also changing, being refined so that they are more accurate. There is no pattern that is set in stone for measuring the value of the pages. By 1996, web masters were figuring out that keywords were important. Remember, at this time, Google was still Backrub and a work in progress. In those days, websites were submitted to Yahoo in the hopes of being indexed by that paramount search engine.

Just a side note, there were other search engines in the very early days such as Wandex, a 1993 entry into the search engine world. It involved a web crawled known as World Wide Web Wanderer. It disappeared over time but another 1993 earch engine, Aliweb, and the 1994 Lycos are still in use. Yahoo offered more and it was the place to be recognized so energetic web masters spammed Yahoo with submissions in the early days. The notion was that the more submissions of s particular site, the more important the big search engine might think it was. For the last years of the 1990s, this was about all there was to SEO.

## PageRank

Google was in the game and by the turn of the century it was becoming the king of algorithm logic for websites. One of the ways it measured successful entrants in the website competitions was with PageRank (PR). This is still a major measurement for websites. PR7 sites are the cream of the crop. A lot of people think that this refers to the ranking of a web page.

It doesn't. PageRank got its name from Larry Page. Google revamped the entire way that websites were ranked with astounding new algorithms. PageRank is a Google trademark and a patented process with Stanford University owning the patent. Google bought the exclusive license rights to the patent. Google gave Stanford 1.8 million shares for the use of these rights.

Page and Brin developed PageRank in 1996 and was based on the concept that link popularity was the best way to measure a website's value. This was back when the men were researching search engines and before they formalized Google. PageRank is at the heart of Google's search engine power.

PageRank is essentially a probability distribution that assesses the probability that someone will randomly reach a particular website. PageRank measures the likelihood by making computations based on iterations of searches. The higher the PageRank, the greater the likelihood that people will find the website.

Early SEO efforts involved using lists of words that were guaranteed to attract the attention of the web crawlers that fed the algorithms. One of the methods that worked for a while was stuffing the meta data with keywords. Other tricks involved using keywords that search engines could see but people could not. There were even sites that included text written in the same color as the background so that the words were there but unseen by website visitors.

A particular method that some people used was to include words such as "sex" which was a highly sought after word. The websites often had nothing to do with sex at all but the web masters believed that if they could get traffic to their websites, people would stay. It was not exactly fair to trick people into landing on a site and soon the big search engine cracked down on keyword stuffing.

## SEO Advice and What Works

This section covers the cutting edge advice for SEO in the first few years of this century. It was accepted and agreed that SEO was the be all and end all when it came to getting traffic to your website. The only real concern that many website owners had was how to get the most traffic for the least cost. Since some of these methods have lost their power, the information in this section are really a bit of a history lesson and not a guide on how to optimize your websites today.

## Link Exchanges

Getting more links into your website was considered a great way to make it look appealing to the search engines which in turn made it look like a great place to visit. After all, a whole lot of other websites liked it well enough to link to it.

## Does this still work?

Yes, if the links are real. That is, these are links that other website owners sought out from you and not links that you purchased from link farms. You can network to get in touch with other pertinent websites to see if they are interested in being associated with you.

## What went wrong?

As Google's algorithms became more astute, they were able to discern which links were authentic links and which ones came from sites that were artificially creating and delivering links. Well, to be accurate, the links were real but they were not high quality. The web sites existed only to provide links so that websites would look like they had hundreds of quality links.

## Keyword Laden Articles

When the need to provide content became important, the chosen method was to have articles on the website. Five or ten articles rich in keywords gave the illusion of value to the site. Writing fast enough to fill up websites was a challenge for many website owners.

Does this still work?

Content is the key to having a great website that Google loves. Good fresh content that is accurate, informative, and current will bring people to visit and return. Using the keyword in the title and first and last paragraph is ideal for good SEO. The emphasis should be on the quality of the writing and the focus on the subject.

What went wrong?

To meet the demand for good web copy, the solution was to use articles from directories or spin articles or outsource the writing.

The problem with directory articles is that over time, these were recognized as duplicate content which took away the value of them as something that would make people come to your website for advice. People who are searching for a topic run a good chance of finding the same content on different websites.

Spun articles are often poor quality. And poor quality is not a way to get people coming back to your site. If you are selling information on your website and your articles are poorly spun, how much confidence is the reader going to have in your offering?

People frequently outsource the writing of their articles and ask for a specific density of keywords. However, sometimes this is not properly rendered and the articles have an unnatural feel to them.

One of the worst mistakes to make is to have a great title and a good lead-in sentence and nothing else. If you go to a website looking for information on a specific topic and you read the title, Seven Great Ways to Lose Weight (for instance) and the first line is "Here are seven great ways to lose weight" you are pleased. But then you read the rest of the articles and aside from having seven points, there is nothing there about losing weight, it is likely that you will never return to that site and for sure you will not sign up for anything that it has to offer.

As for outsourcing, it can be expensive so a lot of web owners try to get a deal and do not pay attention to the quality of the writing.

Example:

This is from an outsourced article on erectile dysfunction. Imagine you are seeking real advice on this issue and you read an article that includes this paragraph:

But before you will use erectile dysfunction cures, it is important that you will seek for medical consultation so that you can get solution from the problem easily. The good thing about prior consultation is that you will also be given with additional non-medication related treatments that can also restore your normal erectile dysfunction problems.

Huh? What does this mean? As a reader, do you really want to waste your time trying to figure out what this nonsense means?

Google changed the algorithm to deal with the immense amount of garbage that was appearing online. Google's mandate is to offer web surfers an easy way to find what they are looking for. When the results are pages and pages of trashy, non-informative, poorly spun crap, Google had to step up and find ways to get through the mass of bad articles.

How to benefit safely?

Have real quality. Write the articles yourself or hire a good writer.

## Google Response to Low Quality

Google's algorithm changes are not something new, as you have seen so far in this book. They are an ongoing effort to keep the search engine relevant for its purpose which is to help people find the information that they want to find. The more threats to this goal, the more diligently Google works to find ways to overcome the threats.

This does not mean that Google is specifically out to get web owners who try to "game" the system. However, in gaming the system with artificial SEO efforts, the end result is usually poor quality websites with the single intention of tricking people into believing the site has authority and valid offerings as shown on Google through PageRank and position. Here are some of the algorithm changes that have taken place in recent years.

## Google Caffeine Algorithm

Caffeine began in August 2009 and put in place in June, 2010. It was a change in Google's architecture which was designed to speed up searches and handle the fast-changing information that comes from places such as Facebook and Twitter. Keywords were given more weight in ranking as was the domain's age. This, like many of the updates in algorithms was merely designed to respond to the changes in how information was being released on the internet.

## Panda Algorithm Update

The Panda update was specifically aimed at so-called thin sites. These are the junkie kind of sites that were SEOed with artificial SEO methods. The change was obvious as news and social networking websites jumped higher in the search engine while sites with mostly advertising plummeted. There were concerns that Google was not able to handle the huge influx of scraper sites and the Panda update was a concerted effort to content with these sites.

The name is not a made up name or an acronym. It came from the engineer who was behind the major new algorithmic change, Navneet Panda.

The effect was dramatic when Panda was rolled out in February 2011 and each time it was tweaked and updated, the ripples continued to be felt in the internet marketing world.

Google blogged about the requirements for a high-quality site, offering the following 23 points (the blog is available at http://googlewebmastercentral.blogspot.com/2 011/05/more-guidance-on-building-high-quality.html):

Would you trust the information presented in this article?

Is this article written by an expert or enthusiast who knows the topic well, or is it more shallow in nature?

Does the site have duplicate, overlapping, or redundant articles on the same or similar topics with slightly different keyword variations?

Would you be comfortable giving your credit card information to this site?

Does this article have spelling, stylistic, or factual errors?

Are the topics driven by genuine interests of readers of the site, or does the site generate content by attempting to guess what might rank well in search engines?

Does the article provide original content or information, original reporting, original research, or original analysis?

Does the page provide substantial value when compared to other pages in search results?

How much quality control is done on content?

Does the article describe both sides of a story?

Is the site a recognized authority on its topic?

Is the content mass-produced by or outsourced to a large number of creators, or spread across a large network of sites, so that individual pages or sites don't get as much attention or care?

Was the article edited well, or does it appear sloppy or hastily produced?

For a health related query, would you trust information from this site?

Would you recognize this site as an authoritative source when mentioned by name?

Does this article provide a complete or comprehensive description of the topic?

Does this article contain insightful analysis or interesting information that is beyond obvious?

Is this the sort of page you'd want to bookmark, share with a friend, or recommend?

Does this article have an excessive amount of ads that distract from or interfere with the main content?

Would you expect to see this article in a printed magazine, encyclopedia or book?

Are the articles short, unsubstantial, or otherwise lacking in helpful specifics?

Are the pages produced with great care and attention to detail vs. less attention to detail?

Would users complain when they see pages from this site?

The entire list of points is reprinted here because this is the essence of what you need to consider in order to have your website thrive online.

Google's Panda used artificial intelligence fed by data from real people who quality tested websites. The changes have been real game-changers for Google search engine optimization techniques. One of the big changes is that PageRank which was there before Google was reduced in its importance in the world of Google search engines. PageRank is important in its own way but once website gurus learned how to trick Google into accepting lower quality websites as high quality entities, it lost a lot of its value. When Panda found pages that were substandard according to its algorithm, it penalized not just the page but the entire website.

Google still runs Panda from time to time to catch the thin sites. By September 2012, Panda was finding fewer and fewer offending pages.

## Penguin Algorithm Update

As part of the ongoing process of keeping Google relevant, in April 2012, Google released its Penguin update. This had an impact on more than three percent of English language search queries. Penguin took direct aim at websites that use black-hat methods for SEO. These include some of the approaches discussed earlier in this book such as link schemes, duplicate content, and keyword stuffing. To state it simply, people who tried to game the search engines were hit hard.

This is a big change from previous algorithm changes which were aimed at best rankings methods and Panda which was aimed at finding a way to demote websites with poor content. Penguin was hitting right at the core of one of the problems which was the use of black-hat SEO.

Just before Penguin, in January 2012, there was a page layout algorithm. It was looking for websites that did not have a lot of content in the area known as above the fold. This refers to the top half of a newspaper, above the place where the papers are folded. This is considered the prime placement in a newspaper. This is the part that is visible when newspapers are sold in boxes or at newsstands. In terms of a website, this is the part of the website that appears on your screen when you load the site into your browser.

### What This Means to the Internet Marketer

Panda and Penguin seem to be poised to stay and other changes are taking place. Here is an example, and if you have studied internet marketing, you may have heard of the power of this technique – exact match domains.

There were courses taught on selling digital products and tangible products using exact match domains. This was the golden secret to achieving a high ranking. Get on page one of Google guaranteed with exact match domain names. This was the battle cry of many people selling advice on how to make it to the top.

If you were selling sewing machines, you didn't want to settle for sewingmachines.com. It was better if you got a domain that had the brand and model name. Singerxx34.com (if Singer had a model xx34) was a better choice. Thousands upon thousands of exact match domains were registered and people worked hard at creating meaningful sites.

Then came the EMD (exact match domain) update. Matt Cutts, known as Google's head of webspam, tweeted it just like this:

Minor weather report: small upcoming Google algo change will reduce low-quality "exact match" domains in search results.

That was at 4:43 pm on September 28, 2012.

The hunt is ongoing and most of what we learned over the past 10 years is no longer valid when it comes to getting highly ranked in Google.

People who were raking it in with their websites suddenly had a rude awakening. Their sites that they had spent thousands raising up in the ranks were suddenly de-indexed. Their websites are gone from Google and no one is able to find them using the good old search engine.

It was a career ender for many in the dedicated world of website marketing. People who were selling tangible products through their exact match domain websites because they were highly ranked for that particular key word saw sales plummet.

The huge legions of SEO writers who were kept busy writing for web owners are finding a change in their work loads too. Fewer web owners are looking for SEO writing because they are confused about the future. The whole game has changed and no one is quite sure what to do.

The big question is:

Is SEO Dead?

The answer may sound confusing but it is both "yes" and "no." SEO as you may know it is dead. If you have a hard drive full of reports on SEO that you carefully collected over the years, you might as well dump them. Google's changes are responding to all the techniques that are the body of those reports. Google knows about the backlinks you can buy on Fiverr or in some of the forums. Google knows about the inaccurate and lightweight articles you can buy for pennies and spin for nothing. They won't let these efforts create a place for you anywhere near the top of Google.

That is the "yes SEO is dead" response.

However, as long as there are search engines, the better tuned a web page is to the search engine's purpose, the better the page will rank – regardless of the algorithm in place. So looking at SEO from this perspective, the response is "No. SEO is not dead."

The rest of this book will look at the best ways to deal with SEO in a positive and productive manner.

### SEO after Panda and Penguin

What can you do moving forward with a new website or with the chore of revamping your current website?

Backlinks

You can still have links on it and to it. You just have to be more discriminating about the links to your site and from your site. Have you heard about the Disavow Tool? This is a new tool that Google offers web publishers so that they can improve their website's quality.

When Google cracked down on poor quality links, a lot of people were caught with the results of backlinks that they bought or gathered from link networks that were less than reputable. Buying links is against the

Google rules but Google reached out to help people who might be caught with links they wish they did not have because these links have caused them to drop from the top of Google.

Google provides the Disavow Tool that lets a web owner report links that they do not want counted on their sites. The effort to have links from another site to your site can be a challenge. Bad link sources may not want to or they may not have the time or resources to remove the thousands of links they have provided over the years. If you disavow the links before your site is penalized for using them, you can save yourself a lot of grief.

If you are looking over your site to streamline it for future success, look at your incoming links to ensure that they are from good sites. If not, you can ask to have them removed by the web owners and if that does not work, you can disavow them.

If you have a lot of links on your blogroll, remove them just in case someone does not like your site and decides to disavow your site. If a site gets a lot of disavow requests, it does not look good for that site and that could cause you problems in the future.

Speaking of bad links in, if you run a site that allows comments, check into making your comments "no follow" because this will keep shabby links from being posted by people who are just looking for link juice. If you have been allowing people to post just to get their links out there for the world to see, the quality of participation might be low. This will decrease your site's value. Clean up those discussion posts and keep them relevant and clean.

### Articles

Go for quality. You don't have to write Pulitzer Prize winning prose. Don't toss out all the keyword SEO information that you have in your head. There are valid reasons for using keywords. Properly used, they do let people know immediately what your site is about.

You don't have to measure the number of words and keywords in an article. It is just a good principle of writing to tell people upfront what the article is about. Use your keyword in the title and in the first paragraph. A rule of thumb is a keyword no more than once every 100 words.

Write with your reader in mind. Really think about what the reader wants. Be personal and open to your readers. Don't follow rigid rules about how long the article should be. Make it valuable. Check your facts. Just because you read it online in someone's blog does not make it a fact.

Be careful when you see ads for new ways to beat the system and rise to page one on Google. You can bet that Google will soon see any signs of news ways to get around the changes and once again have flimsy sites rise to the top and pull the plug on that method too.

Flimsy sites are those that offer nothing new and interesting. It is the nature of some sites that there is not a great deal of information available because you are offering a service such as, for instance, computer repair.

You can provide a lot of information but people coming to your site don't necessarily want to read all about what might be wrong with their computer or how to fix it themselves. They want to know if you can fix it and how long it will take and how much it will cost.

Your site might not have a lot of content but it is a real site offering a real service and it can be optimized for your specific business and location so that if someone searches for Joe's computer repair in Lower Baddeck they will be able to find it because if it is properly SEOed, you will have that information included in the keywords on the site. You don't need to be at the top of the search engines for computer repairs anywhere on the planet. You just need to be found by someone in Lower Baddeck looking for a computer repair person.

Optimizing your website for successful search engine results is all about providing quality. You are not limited to writing. More and more, video is becoming the way to appeal to people. You can add video to your site and have the written version there as well as the video. This appeals to those who like to read and to those who like the visual aspect.

Organize your site so that it easy for people to find things. Even if you have great articles and content, if there is no way for people to find their way from one article or post to the next one, they will become frustrated and leave, never to return.

Post to your site consistently. If you have a blog and only blog one in a while with no consistent pattern, you will have a hard time getting people to return. If you have evergreen content rather than a blog, check it from time to time to make sure all links are working and that the information is still relevant.

## Conclusion

This has been a journey through how the World Wide Web works and why search engines are so powerful. Specifically this has been an explanation of why Google is so powerful.

It would be great if there was a way to outline the steps to take that would put your website at the top of the search engines. For the past 10 to 12 years, there have been guides to making your website reach the number one spot and for many people, these methods did work for a little while.

The online world is a very fast-paced environment. People are in a rush to find what they want to find and people are in a rush to get their pages online and in front of interested eyes. The faster that the demand for information grew, the more urgently web publishers sought shortcuts to meeting these demands.

Software was developed to do everything from spin articles to assess your keywords to scrape content to create and post your blogs. Outsourcing became an essential part of doing online business.

The whole framework was in place and a new service industry grew up and while this way of doing business seemed to be permanently in place, this is a very volatile industry. Successful entrepreneurs are those who can focus on a clear goal and find ethical and durable ways to create their online presence.

The rules for SEO are much simpler but this does not mean that the work is much easier. You have to work a little harder to provide the kind of quality that Google demands.

### Quick SEO Guidelines

Write interesting articles and blogs that make you look real and knowledgeable.

Use keywords sparingly but use them.

Clean up your backlinks so your site does not suffer from being disavowed.

Check the links left on your site to make sure
that they are not the cause of poor quality
comments.

# Amanda's Other Books:

## Economic Crisis: World Food System - The Battle against Poverty, Pollution and Corruption

## Flood Your Websites and Blogs with Free Traffic: Quickly Learn How to Send Visitors to Your Web Sites the Organic Way

## Anti-Aging Guide Top Tips: Inspiration and Helpful Advice to Help You Feel Gorgeous and Look Younger

# Home Quick Makeovers Top Tips: Learn How to Design, Decorate and Furnish Your Ideal Home.

If you would like to share this book with another person, please purchase an additional copy for each recipient. Thank you for respecting the hard work of this author.

Thank you for downloading the book - Small Business: Quick and Easy Guide to Marketing, Business and the Digital Generation - 2 Book Bundle.

www.ingramcontent.com/pod-product-compliance
Lightning Source LLC
Chambersburg PA
CBHW072308200526
45168CB00014B/891